D0290526

Modernism Past and Future
モダニズムのこれまでとこれから

Collected Essays
エッセイ集

Eizo Nishio

Art & Books

Contents

Modernism: Past and Future

Modernism: Past and Future

Over the course of human history since the Renaissance, advances in science and humanities have continued to expand our sphere of activity and provide greater individual freedom. Over time, this has brought an end to absolute monarchies and led to the emergence of democratic societies. The history of art has also taken shape within this overall context.

A prime example can be seen in the development of realism in painting. Realism can be taken to refer to either a realistic feel or a precise style of painting. In either case however, the realist way of viewing things stems from considerable advances in self-consciousness, coming from the same standpoint as the anti-monarchy movement. Under an absolute monarchy, there are simply too many contradictions for things to be viewed realistically.

In contrast, painting under an absolute monarchy is characterized by embellishment. There are other paintings that give a very personal insight into the artist through their individual imagination, they are not directly linked to the flow of history.

Democracy started to become a reality in the 19th century and came to fruition in the 20th century with the establishment of countless democratic nations. The characteristics of 20th century art that most reflect this process are abstract art and Modernism.

Abstract art tends to be regarded as something that isn't representational, something far removed from realism. As works are composed of recognizable shapes and colors however, they essentially represent without illusionism. In that respect, abstract art contains elements of realism that go beyond conventional realism. This also indicates that the viewer has undergone major changes to feel that artwork is real and find value in it. With that in mind, it would be fair to say that abstract art is just another new form of realism that emerged after the start of the 20th century.

The other key characteristic of 20th century art is Modernism, which is a mood and order into visual culture that captures the euphoria and vitality of life in the democratic nation. In that respect, Modernism extends far beyond abstract art, which is just one form of expression. Modernism is not just a 20th century phenomenon. It can be traced back to any country in history that established a democratic approach to politics, no matter how incomplete, going all the way back to Ancient Greece, let alone the Renaissance.

Although Modernism is sometimes regarded as synonymous with abstract art, it actually includes representational painting and all other forms of art that capture that same mood. There is one major hole in the argument that Modernism is the same as abstract art, namely that there are forms of expression that are abstract without being modernist. This is typically illustrated by the architecture under fascist dictatorships during World War II or under communist regimes. Buildings were stripped of all embellishments and simplified using straight lines. This deformed type of expression on a massive scale is the simplest, most effective means of visual expression, taking the sense of euphoria from Modernism and adding an overbearing dose of sanctity. In prewar Japan too, huge torii gates were used as state-sanctioned symbols of Shintoism designed to boost national prestige.

Unlike forms of expression such as this, modernist expression inevitably creates a positive sense of individual humanity. Entasis pillars in Greek architecture are a prime example of this, with their gentle swelling and vertical embellishment.

The fact that the Russian Avant-Garde movement and Abstract

Expressionism emerged separately in the Soviet Union and the United States is no coincidence. Divided along the lines between capitalism and communism, these two superpowers led the way for most of 20th century. Apart from the early years, the Soviet Union was a dictatorship that collapsed in 1991. In spite of differences in terminology, with the Soviet Union governed by the workers for the workers and the United States by the people for the people, and in the way in which these two superpowers achieved their goals, they both had philosophies that were essentially similar and inevitably adhered to Modernism, based on people from all over both nations coming together in the name of progress. In the Soviet Union in particular, the fact that state did not even allow religion gave rise to a purified form of Modernism, as typified by Malevich's square painting. As that struggled to gain acceptance straight away in the Soviet Union however, there was a shift towards formal Socialist Realist painting from the Stalin era onwards.

Postwar American Abstract Expressionist painting was also based strictly on Modernism. The contrasting use of freehand lines and a wider range of colors however found acceptance and have continued to develop into a sustainable form of expression, paving the way for more free-form practices such as Color Field painting or Shaped Canvas.

After the war, the center of the art world shifted to the United States, ushering in a fully-fledged era of Modernism from the 1940s to the 1970s. Although the 1980s saw the arrival of so-called Post-Modernism, this was just a limited movement that was essentially Modernism with the addition of such as problematic architectural embellishments or New Painting motifs. Post-Modernism is essentially a popularized extension of Modernism.

Since the days of large-scale computers in the 1980s, personal computers have become commonplace, enabling anyone to easily access information via the internet. Reflecting such an era, formal Modernism has evolved into a popularized form of Modernism and has become a more integral part of our everyday lives today. As Modernism continues to evolve, it is increasingly spreading out around the globe, in line with the emergence of new economic powers in other parts of the world.

With more and more democracies springing up all over the world, democracy is likely to become a more or less universal political regime in the future. Even so, each new era will bring with it new threats to democracy. The disappearance of anti-democratic forces will make democracy itself, and its central essence, harder to distinguish. This will make it difficult to clearly define and maintain a continual awareness of democracy. At this point, preventing democracy from descending into a grey area is likely to become a top priority.

Art always reflects the hopes of the current era. Although it may seem like art is leading the way, it is in fact reacting passively to current events. To put it another way, you could say that the function of art is to take stock of the current era and to help establish it in a cultural context. During good times, art helps lay the foundations for better times, but the reverse is also true. As a grey area begins to open up within democracy in the future, the art world is likely to find it harder and harder to determine what constitutes good art. It needs to be determined on the basis of Modernism, the fundamental language in the visual culture of democracy. Even today, democracy runs the risk of falling into a mobocrary or, somewhat less likely, totalitarianism under the control of a government of right- or left-wing party. Anyone involved in the art world take great care and strive to sharpen their eyes to truly discern the works of art in the day when there is an increase in expression that is underpinned by excessive extravagance and embellishment or a sense of emptiness as exceeding minimalism, even if it seems to have purity, so that the art world will move in a better direction wherever possible. This matter will be an important responsibility for everyone involved in the art world in the future.

I can but hope that Modernism will remain buoyant and positive in the future and that art will continue to evolve stably in line with the current era.

December 2017

モダニズムのこれまでとこれから

モダニズムのこれまでとこれから

ルネッサンス以降の人類の歴史は、自然科学と人文科学の発展が個人に活動領域の広がりと自由をもたらし、やがて絶対王制を脱して民主主義社会の実現に至る過程であり、美術の歴史もこの大きな流れの中にあります。

このことは、絵画においてはリアリズムの発展に見ることが出来ます。リアリズムとは、リアルに感じられる、と、正確に描く、の両義があります。が、いずれの場合でも、このような物事の捉え方は自我の著しい進捗（しんちょく）であり、反王制的な立場に違いはありません。絶対王制は、リアルに捉えられるには矛盾が多すぎるのです。

反対に、絶対王制の絵画を特徴付けるものは装飾性です。また、絵画にはこれ以外に、極めて私的な世界である個人的なイマジネーションの発露としての絵画がありますが、それは歴史の流れとは直接的な関係はありません。

民主主義は19世紀にその現実的な姿を現し、20世紀において多くの民主主義国家の成立により完全に具現化しました。こうした流れを反映しての、20世紀の美術における最大の特徴は、抽象とモダニズムにあります。

抽象は一般的に、再現的なものではないので、リアリズムとは違うものと捉えられがちですが、そこには見たままの形と色彩のみがある、つまり、イリュージョニズムを排して絵画は成立しているのであり、この点において、従来のリアリズムより、よりリアリズムであり、また同時に、見る側が、それをリアルに感じ価値を見出すまでに大きく変化したことも意味します。このことから、抽象は20世紀に入って生み出されたリアリズムのもう一つの新しい形態と言えます。

一方、20世紀美術のもう一つの大きな特徴であるモダニズムは、民主主義国家の市民が高揚感と活力をもっていきいきと生活するための、

ヴィジュアル・カルチャーにおけるムードであり規律です。そういった意味では、表現の一形態である完全抽象を越えて、モダニズムは遙かに大きな広がりを持っています。また、モダニズムは、20世紀だけではなく、歴史上、不完全ではあっても民主的政治形態が存在した国々において、ルネッサンスはおろかギリシャ文明までも遡ることが出来ます。

モダニズムは、抽象と同義に捉えられる場合もありますが、具象絵画を始め、そういったムードを持つすべてのアートを含みます。モダニズム＝抽象、と捉えていると、そこには大きな落とし穴があります。抽象であってもモダニズムではない表現が存在するからです。それは第二次大戦中のファッシズムの独裁国家や共産主義体制下における建築などに典型的に見ることが出来、一切の装飾性を排して直線で単純化され、デフォルメにより巨大化された表現は、モダニズムから高揚感のみを取り出して威圧的な神聖さを加味するのに最も簡単で効果的なヴィジュアル面での方法です。戦前の日本においても、国威発揚のために国家神道のシンボルとしての巨大な鳥居が利用されました。
こういった表現に対し、モダニズムの表現には必ず個人の人間性に対するプラス面が感じられ、それは例えばギリシャ建築のエンタシスにおける緩い膨らみと縦筋の装飾などに見ることが出来ます。

ロシアン＝アヴァンギャルドと抽象表現主義がソビエト連邦とアメリカに出現したのは別に偶然のことではありません。この2つの大国は、資本主義と共産主義の2つの陣営に分かれ、共に20世紀をリードして来ました。ソビエト連邦はその初期を除き、独裁体制になり、そして1991年に終焉を迎えましたが、この2つの大国は共に、片や、労働者による労働者のための政治、片や、人民による人民のための政治、と言葉は違っていても、また実現した形においては違ったけれども、その理念においては本質的に似ており、巨大な国の市民が一丸となって前進するために必然的にモダニズムの規律が求められました。特にソビエト連邦においては、体制が宗教をも認めないために、モダニズムの純化された形－マレーヴィッチの方形の絵画－を生み出し、しかしそれ

はまたソビエトにおいても直ちに受け入れることが出来なかったために、スターリン時代以降、形式的なソーシャリスト・リアリズム絵画に変化して行きました。

これに対し、戦後のアメリカ抽象表現主義絵画は、厳格なフォーマル・モダニズムではありましたが、より自由で手触りのある線や色彩により、人々が受け入れ、持続可能な表現として、その後の、にじみや形態の自由さを持ったカラー・フィールド・ペインティングや、シェイプト・カンバス絵画に引き継がれてゆきます。

戦後、アートはその中心を完全にアメリカに移し、1940年代から1970年代まで名実共にモダニズムの時代を迎えます。1980年代以降はポスト・モダニズムが言われますが、そこで問題になる建築の装飾性やニュー・ペインティングのモチーフも、モダニズムに加味された限定的な動きで、本質的にはモダニズムであり、その延長線上にあるポピュラリゼイション化したモダニズムと言えます。

大型コンピューターが主役の時代から、1980年代以降、パーソナル・コンピューターが一般化し、誰でもネットを通じて情報を手に入れられる時代の反映として、フォーマルなモダニズムが、より身近なものに変化して来た訳です。こうしてモダニズムは変化しつつ、欧米だけでなく、経済の多極化と共に世界中に広がりつつあります。

現在、民主主義は世界中に広がり、今後、ほぼ世界中が一応、民主主義の政治形態をとるようになるでしょう。しかし、おそらく民主主義はその時から新しい危機にさらされることになります。反民主主義的なものが消えることにより、民主主義そのものが、あるいはその中心が見えにくくなる、といったことが起こり、民主主義というものをはっきりと、そして常に認識することが難しくなるためです。そしてこの時点からおそらく民主主義のグレーゾーンへのチェックが最も大きな問題となって来ます。

アートは常に時代の希望を反映するものなので、アートは時代をリー

ドしているように見えても実は時代に沿って受動的に動くものです。別の言い方をすれば、アートは、時代を認識し文化面において、その時代を定着させて行く作業と言えます。良い時代にはより良く時代を補強しますが、その逆もまたあり得ます。今後、民主主義のグレーゾーンが広がるにつれ、アートの世界でも、どういったアートが良いものであるかについての判断がより一層難しくなることが予想されます。モダニズムは、民主主義におけるヴィジュアル面での基本言語ですので、それを基準に判断する必要があります。現在でも民主主義は、衆愚政治、また可能性は低いにせよ、右翼政権、左翼政権による全体主義に陥る危険性にさらされています。過度な華美や装飾、また、ミニマリズムを越えるような、純粋さは感じられても虚無感が支配するような表現が多くなる時代には、より注意を払い、選別眼を厳しくして、アートを少しでも良い方向へ向けることは、今後のアート関係者の大事な責任となると思います。

今後も、快活で前向きなモダニズムの中で、アートが時代と共に、安定的、継続的に発展していくことを願って止みません。

December 2017

About Minimal Art

About Minimal Art

When I think about the origin of minimal art, I cannot help but imagine Brancusi's sculpture and Malevich's square painting.

Brancusi was the sculptor who moved from half-abstractionism to total abstractionism and Malevich created paintings resonating with energy during a revolutionary period.

Because minimal art was based on the anti-emotional intellectual aesthetic during the process by which materialistic civilization maturing further into a stable society in the late 20th century, it was naturally different from the works by creators in the early 20th century.

What was the origin of minimal art? I think that minimal art came from a sculpture titled *Here I* by Barnett Newman in 1950 and his paintings.

I have the impression that minimal art significantly jumped from there to Donald Judd, Carl Andre and Walter de Maria. It was, so to speak, a jump from individualism to holism, but a large space remained in between. Tony Smith, Richard Serra and Ulrich Rueckriem produced great performances in this area and Sol LeWitt and Dan Flavin are also active. Robert Smithson and Richard Long are closely related here, too.

What is minimal painting? How is minimal painting which is paintings without any remnants of the painters' technique and different from geometric abstraction?

There are still many untouched aspects in this area that involve huge possibilities.

Quite a few artists' works tend to have the style of minimal art, if you see it as a tendency toward simplification and reduction while setting aside the sense of minimal expression.

In this context, minimal tendency can mean the hidden current of art in the latter 20th century, and the advent of minimal art is its natural course. It coincides with the general flow of modern life.

I am very interested in the diversity of minimal art.

January 2017

ミニマル・アートについて

ミニマル・アートについて

ミニマル・アートの始まりを考える時、ブランクーシの彫刻や、マレーヴィッチの方形の絵画がふと思い浮かびます。

ですが、ブランクーシは半抽象から完全抽象への道を追求した彫刻家であり、マレーヴィッチは革命期のエネルギーに共振して絵画を制作しました。

ミニマル・アートは、20 世紀後半の安定した社会の中で、物質文明がより成熟していく過程での、反情緒的、理知的美意識に立脚していますので、20 世紀前半の作家の作品とは自ずと異なります。

では、ミニマル・アートが直接的にどこから始まったかと言うと、それは、バーネット・ニューマンの 1950 年の彫刻 "Here Ⅰ" と彼の絵画からだと思います。

そしてここからドナルド・ジャッド、カール・アンドレ、ウォルター・デ・マリアに一気にジャンプしている感があります。いわば、個から全一性（ホーリズム）へのジャンプですが、その間に大きな空間が残されました。トニー・スミスやリチャード・セラ、ウーリッヒ・リュックリームが、この領域で活動しており、ソル・ルウィット、ダン・フレヴィンはこの領域でも活動しています。ロバート・スミッソン、リチャード・ロングも関係の深い作家です。

ミニマル絵画とは何でしょうか？
画家の手業を残さず、幾何学的抽象とも違うミニマル絵画とは？

この領域にはまだまだ未踏の地が多く、これから大きな可能性を持った場所です。

また、ミニマル・アートを、最小限の表現という定義から離れて、その単純化、簡素化の傾向に注目すると、実に多くのアーティストがこの傾向を持っています。

そう考えると、ミニマルな傾向は 20 世紀後半のアートの隠された潮流
であり、ミニマル・アートの出現はその当然の帰結である、と言えま
す。
これは現代生活の一般的な流れとも合致しています。

私はミニマル・アートの多様性に大いに興味を持っています。

January 2017

Japanese History and Contemporary Art

Japanese History and Contemporary Art

The history of Japan can be divided broadly into four periods: the period ruled by tenno (Japanese emperor), in which a deep connection existed with religion, the period in which samurai came to power, the period between the Meiji Restoration and pre-war and the modern post-war period. The greatest changes in history occurred during the period between pre-war and post-war Japan, which resulted in a paradigm shift.

One of the most significant characteristics that can be observed in the history of Japan is that the period ruled by tenno and samurai (military government) was very long, without any sudden revolt initiated by the citizens. The connection between the Restoration of Imperial Rule and the modern state remained strong well into the Meiji era, leaving little to develop until the change in the post-war political system when democracy was established. Only after this point did a huge and sudden paradigm shift occur in society.

Over 70 years have passed since the end of the war, and Japan is now a G7 member. On the surface, Japan appears to be the same as any Western country. However, the effect of the historic change remains within the country to this very day. While the difference between the outside and inside is not as significant as it was during the immediate post-war period, a complex inner structure still exists that completely differs from the outside world in the Japanese consciousness.

I believe that the largest changes in the history of Japan occurred before and after the war. However, a quite long period of time will be required until such an understanding of history can be established.

Art is a part of society and therefore it reflects events that occurred throughout history as well as in the social consciousness. The art of modern Japan is intermingled with Japanese as well as Western-style paintings from the pre-war period, contemporary art from the post-war period, along with art from America and Europe. Many art museums collect works of art based on such classifications. However, contemporary art in Japan still differs from that in the West, both in terms of perception as well as structure, reflecting our modern society as a whole.

I would like to put classic art aside and focus on contemporary art. Similar to Japan's history, I believe that a quite long period of time will be required until the difference in perception between Japanese contemporary art and that of America and Europe disappears. The parties concerned are required to familiarize themselves with the global situation and make persistent efforts until it is materialized.

Artists eventually leave their home region and country to experience other forms of art that are available throughout the world. The majority of the world's art has become standardized. I mentioned earlier that the difference between Japanese art and that of the West would remain for a quite long period of time. However, Japanese art has started to merge with Western art. Japanese artists are required to pay attention to commonalities in the world to create works of art that reflect these traits. "Typically Japanese" works of art no longer exist. Still, it is natural for viewers to sense such quality in the background. I believe that maintaining this point of view is the best form of education for future artists, although I fully appreciate that doing so is difficult.

Nonverbal culture was established during the period when the government was ruled by tenno. Shintoism do not have a sacred scripture. Samurai honored their own view of life and death. Even though void or emptiness is one of characteristics observed in Japanese culture, I do not like emphasizing these characteristics in expression.

Minimalism, which is created using minimal expression, is different from a concept of that in Japan. Art is a form of work produced in society and therefore it must provide the citizens with energy and some sort of benefit. Although void or emptiness is characteristics observed in Japanese culture, I do not agree with expressing a sense of emptiness for viewers to see. Japanese artists must not forget this point.

May 2017

日本の歴史と現代アート

日本の歴史と現代アート

日本の歴史を考えると、宗教と強く結び付いた天皇制、武家政権、明治維新から戦前、戦後現代社会、の 4 期に大きく分けることが出来ます。
この歴史の中で一番大きな変化は、戦前から戦後への変化で、非常に大きな断層がそこにあります。

日本の歴史の中で一つ顕著なことは、天皇制から武家政権＝軍事政権までが余りに長すぎたために、市民社会の勃興が見られず、明治時代になっても王政復古が近代国家と強く結び付いていたために、その発展が未熟なままに、戦後の民主主義、市民社会にいっぺんに大きなパラダイム・シフトが起きた、という点です。

戦後 70 年以上経過して、日本も G7 の一員となり、欧米諸国と外見上差異はなくなりました。ですが、この歴史上の巨大な断層は、内面的にまだ大きく影響しており、戦後間もない頃と比べると現在その差は非常に小さくなっているとはいえ、未だ外見とは違った複雑な意識構造が残っています。

私は、戦前と戦後が日本の歴史における最大の変化点だと考えています。ですが、そのような歴史認識がなされるには、今後相当な年月を要することとなるでしょう。

美術は社会の一部ですから、こういった歴史上の事柄、社会意識がすべて反映されます。現在の日本の美術状況は、戦前からの日本画、洋画、戦後の現代美術、アメリカ、ヨーロッパの美術、が混在しています。多くの美術館もこれに沿ったコレクションがなされています。
日本で現代美術と言っても、現在の欧米のアートとは認識、構造の面でまだまだ違いが目立ちます。それは社会のあり方をそのまま反映しています。

古典美術は別として、現代のアートと言った時に、アメリカ、ヨーロッパとその認識の差異がなくなるのは歴史同様、相当な年月を要すると思いますが、関係者は世界の情報を広く取り、その差異がなくなるまでの不断の努力が必要です。

アーティストは、それぞれの国、地域から出発して、やがて世界のアートに触れてゆきます。
現在の世界のアートは、ほぼ共通化されています。まだまだ違いがある、と述べましたが、日本もその一部に入りつつある時代でもあると思います。
あくまでも世界の共通項に目を向けて、それに沿ったアートを目指さなければなりません。
日本人らしい、あるいは日本らしいアート、というものは既に存在していません。しかし、作品の背後にそのことが感じられるのは自然なことです。
難しいことですが、この認識がこれからのアーティストの一番の素養となると思います。

天皇制は言葉を発しない文化です。神道には教典はありません。武士道には独特の死生観があります。
空、無、ということは、日本文化の大きな特質の一つなのですが、この点を表現に強調することには感心しません。

ミニマリズムは、最小限の表現ですので、このこととは異なります。
アートは、社会の仕事の一つですから、そこに活力や何らかのプラスの面を与える必要があります。
空や無が日本文化の特質の一つであると言っても、見るものに空虚感や虚無感を与えることは良いことだとは思いません。
日本人の表現者はこの点を忘れないようにしなければなりません。

May 2017

Modern Japanese Society and the Tenno System
(Japanese emperor system)

Modern Japanese Society and the Tenno System (Japanese emperor system)

The country name "Japan" does not reveal its system of government. So what is Japan's system of government? In fact it is a democracy, which recognizes the tenno as a symbol of the state.

The Constitution of Japan stipulates that the tenno shall be the symbol of the state and that sovereign power resides with the people. Tenno is not actually a monarch but a symbol. The tenno system can be said to be a weak form of constitutional monarchy. Since the Constitution does not include the word "monarch," Japan does not have one.

What is a democracy? It is difficult to define it, but one of the most critical requirements is that there be no hereditary echelon in the nation's organization.

From this standpoint, Japan cannot formally be described as a pure democracy. However, no one would probably dispute the fact that post-war Japan is essentially a democratic nation, and yet the tenno system is managed by a governmental organization, the Imperial Household Agency, and the scale of the system makes the tenno look like a constitutional monarch rather than a symbol. The Imperial Household Agency is allocated a total annual budget in the region of ¥26.1 billion yen (FY2009) (*1). This is equivalent to around 1.7 times the total salaries of all members of both the upper and lower houses of the National Diet of Japan.

The roles of the tenno are limited to ceremonial duties only under the Constitution of Japan. However, medals of honor and awards have been expanded beyond the limit, and expenses for the tenno system has increased dramatically from the time when the system that recognizes the tenno as a symbol of the state started after World War II.

I believe that this situation is the main reason why Japanese people cannot confidently say that Japan is a true democracy.

According to the results of a 2009 opinion survey (*2), 8% of respondents supported the abolition of the Tenno system, which is not an insignificant number by any means. The pros and cons of the symbolic Emperor system have never been put up for public discussion since it was introduced after the end of the Second World War. For Japan to become a true democracy, the tenno system needs to be abolished or, at the very least, placed outside the government framework. But it seems extremely unlikely that Japan will see any amendments to its constitution in this regard any time soon.

But since there is now actually only one boy in the next generation with the right of succession to the Imperial throne, I think that, if things kept going the way they are, this system would die out naturally. However, attempts are likely be made to maintain the system by allowing a female tenno. Even so, given its dwindling size, the Imperial Family no doubt faces tough times ahead. Supposing a female tenno was allowed, if the all-male lineage was interrupted, the tradition of *bansei ikkei* or patrilineal succession, which lies at the very core of the tenno system, would collapse, and this would, in fact, mark the end of the tenno system in its original form. From this point onward, the tenno system would lose its meaning and exist in name only. In other words, the belief in the divinity of direct male descendants, which is fundamental to the tenno system, would collapse, meaning that the tenno is no longer divine. This would drive away many politicians, academics and bureaucrats with an Emperor-centric ideology and would also change the tenno's relationship with religion (*3).

The tenno has also had a huge impact on *seken* or the community in Japan (*4). It is this community which has harbored a deep sense of awe, albeit nothing compared to that in prewar Japan. However, this sense of awe also appears to be decreasing these days compared to the Showa Era, as the community diminishes and urban mentality becomes more firmly established.

Japan has undergone a huge transformation between the prewar and postwar periods. The shift to democracy after the war, moving away from a system which began in the Meiji Era with the restoration of Imperial Rule and lasted until the end of the war, was such a huge change. The Meiji Constitution (Constitution of the Empire of Japan), which was enacted in the Meiji period and which was in force until immediately after the end of the war, reflected the characteristics of absolute monarchism too strongly. Under the constitution, the Emperor had the right to make all legislative, executive, and judiciary decisions. The constitution had no provisions for a prime minister or cabinet. The military was under the supreme command of the Emperor.

Japan took the form of a constitutional monarchy. However, considering the situation described above, we have to say that it was different from the constitutional monarchy in Europe, where the king's power was limited by parliament.

Since ancient times, the tenno had occupied the position of primacy in the Japanese nation and yet had had no direct involvement in politics to a degree unparalleled in the world. This remained the same even after the Meiji Era. Consequently, the form of government under the tenno system appeared less authoritarian, prompting some to mistakenly believe that the system was democratic. However, the ambiguities of the tenno system, among which the tenno was not involved in politics while being a towering figure, caused a huge power vacuum and uncertainty over where responsibility lay. This resulted in the military invoking the divine will of the tenno and running amok without any intervention in World War II.

Following Japan's defeat, the Constitution of Japan was established under the American Occupation. Consisting of eleven Chapters, this Constitution deals with the Emperor in the opening first chapter, with Article 1 stating that the Emperor shall be the symbol of the State and that sovereign power resides in the People, and Articles 3, 4 and 7 providing for the acts of the Emperor in matters of state and restrictions thereon, in other words, stating that the Emperor shall perform only acts in matters of state, that all such acts in matter of states shall require the advice and approval of the Cabinet, and that the Emperor shall not have powers related to government. These provisions about the Emperor at the start of the Constitution are considered to have placed strong restrictions on the acts of the Emperor in light of the experiences of the war. The Constitution of Japan includes acts in matters of state that give a peculiar impression in terms of the description in Article 1 of the Constitution of Japan that sovereignty resides in the people, even though all of these acts require the advice and approval of the Cabinet. Such acts in matters of state include, among others, the convocation of the Diet, appointment of ministers of state and announcement of national elections, all of which are basis of democracy. Even countries that are constitutional monarchies do not have provisions like these. It is commonly accepted that the contentious Article 9 expressly renouncing war and laying down arms was proposed by the Japanese side to preserve the tenno system which was under criticism from other countries. Thus, the Constitution of Japan was born and, dubbed the Peace Constitution, it has fortunately survived to the present day thanks to maintenance of the Western world order built on US power.

The Constitution says that the Emperor shall be the symbol of the State and of the unity of the People, but when we say that a person is a symbol, as stipulated in the Constitution, what does this mean? Things like national flags and national anthems are determined specifically by law, and there are no other examples, anywhere in the world, of a person being identified as a symbol in the Constitution. Usually, a symbol is something other than a person, such as national flag or a national emblem, something to which no-one has any particular objection. Regarding the use of a specific individual as a symbol would mean a personality to which none of the people in the country would object and that would be respected. However, even the Emperor has a personality of his own and would therefore be required to refrain from making direct remarks in order to maintain the authority that is expected of an individual in his position. The prime ministers and presidents who are the leaders of modern-day democracies need to speak eloquently at all times. People in all walks of life are allowed to actively express their views and pursue self-fulfillment. On the other hand, the Emperor is guaranteed an important position without officially uttering any word.

The tenno system and democracy are completely contradictory. In my view, leaving the unexplainable contradiction unaddressed could quite negatively affect the development of logical thinking among the people.

*1 : Calculated based on the table of trends in the budget of the Imperial Household Agency on the agency's website and other data.

*2 : Based on NHK's opinion poll conducted in November 2009

*3 : The tenno has been deeply linked with *Shinto* since the early days of the family. When, in the Meiji Era, the legendary *Amaterasu* (Sun Goddess) was uniformly determined as the most important deity of *Shinto*, the government created the State *Shinto* system, elevating the tenno, who was considered a direct descendant of *Amaterasu*, to divine status. After the war, separation of religion and politics took place, but there is still a strong awareness of the tenno as the central presence in the *Shinto* religion and this stems from the divinity of the tenno passed through the blood line of emperors (*bansei–ikkei*).

*4 : In Japan, the differences between *seken* (community) and *shakai* (society) are unclear, but there are differences between the two. The Japanese political system changed rapidly from military rule in the Edo period to a modern state in the Meiji period. For this reason, it can be said that a closed village mentality and the mentality of townspeople who lived in small communities began to be applied to Japanese society as a whole during this period of transition and survived after the Meiji period. *Seken* represents this concept of closed human relationships between people who share the same identity. Generally speaking, the *seken* mentality is easily swayed by authority and is averse to being different from others. *Shakai* refers to a collection of people who share an urban mentality, and who have more autonomy and a broader awareness.

September 2017

現代日本社会と天皇制

現代日本社会と天皇制

日本は国の政体を国名として表記していません。
では、現代の日本は一体どういった政体かと言えば、それは、象徴天皇制を内に抱えた民主制であると言えます。

憲法に天皇は象徴であり主権は国民に存する、と明記されていますので、天皇は君主ではなく、あくまでも象徴です。立憲君主制がさらに弱まった形と言ってよいと思います。君主という記載はありませんので、君主は存在していません。

民主主義が何かというのは難しい問題を含んでいますが、その必須条件の一つは国の組織の内部に世襲により固定化された階層がないということです。この点から言うと、形としては日本は純粋な民主主義国家とは言えません。但し、戦後の日本は実質的には民主主義の国家であり、その事に異議を唱える人は居ないと思いますが、現在でも天皇制は宮内庁という確固とした政府組織により運営されており、象徴というよりはあたかも立憲君主制であるかのような規模で維持されています。宮内庁の年間予算は関連予算を含め年間 261 億円（2009 年度）（注 1）、という規模で維持されており、これは日本の国会の衆参両院議員すべての給与の約 1.7 倍に相当します。憲法に規定された天皇の仕事は限定的な儀式、儀礼的なことだけのはずですが、現在はこの範囲を越えて褒章、叙勲行事の拡大などにより、戦後の象徴天皇制が始まった当初と比べるとその費用は格段に増大しています。こうした状況が、国民が民主主義について考えた場合、日本が真の民主主義国家であると自信を持って言うことの妨げとなっている大きな理由であると思います。
2009 年のアンケート（注 2）によれば、その 8%が「天皇制を廃止する」と回答しています。これは決して小さい数字ではありません。戦後、象徴天皇制が始まって以来、その是非は一度も問われた事がありません。日本が真の民主主義国家になるためには、天皇制を廃止するか少

なくとも天皇制は政府の外部に設置するべきですが、この点について近い将来、憲法改正が日本で行われる可能性は非常に低いと思われます。

ただ、実際には、皇位継承権を持つ次世代の男子は現在 1 人だけですので、この制度はこのまま行くと自然消滅ということになると思いますが、恐らく女性天皇を認めるということで制度の維持が図られると思われます。その場合でも、皇族数が少ないためにその将来は厳しいものと思われます。こうして女性天皇が認められるにしても、もし男子天皇の系譜が途切れた場合には、天皇制の持つ最も重要な核である「万世一系」の伝統が崩れることになり、実際には本来の天皇制はその時点で終了となります。その後の天皇制は形式的なものとなります。このことはどういうことかと言えば、直系男子の中に神性が宿るという天皇制の最も基本的な考え方があり、それが崩れる、つまり神性が失われるという事です。これに伴い、天皇が国の中心であると考えている政治家、学者、官僚の多くは離れて行き、また、宗教との関係（注3）も変わって行くと予想されます。

また、天皇はいわゆる「世間」（注 4）にも大きな影響を与えていました。戦前とは比べようもありませんが、畏れの意識を大きく持っていたのがこの世間です。しかし、それも昭和天皇の時代から比べると現在では世間がより小さくなり、市民意識が定着していく中で減少していると思われます。

戦前から戦後にかけては非常に大きな変化がありました。王政復古による明治時代に始まり終戦まで続いた体制から、戦後民主主義体制へという余りにも大きな変化です。明治期に制定され第 2 次世界大戦の終わりまで続いた明治憲法（大日本帝国憲法）は立法、行政、司法の決定権がすべて天皇にあり、首相、内閣の規定がなく軍の統帥権も天皇にあるなど絶対王政の要素が強過ぎるものでした。この時代は形としては立憲君主制の形態を取ってはいましたが、議会が王に制限を加えるヨーロッパの立憲君主制とは異なったものであったと言わざるを

得ません。

古来より、天皇は国の中央に位置しながら世界でも類がない程、政治を直接行って来ませんでした。明治期以降においてもそれは変わっていません。この事から、天皇制の下での政治形態は独裁的な印象が薄くなり、その点をもってして民主主義的であったと誤解される場合がありますが、何も政治は行わないが巨大であるという天皇制の持つ曖昧さは、必然的に大きな権力の空白と責任の所在の不明確さをもたらし、それは第 2 次世界大戦において神である天皇の意に沿っているとして軍部が他の機関からの干渉を受けることなく暴走する結果を招きました。

日本の敗戦後、占領国アメリカにより日本国憲法が制定されました。11章から成るこの憲法は、始めの第 1 章が天皇に関することであり、第 1 条の、天皇は日本国の象徴であり主権は国民に存する、と 3,4,7 条が天皇の国事行為とその制限、つまり国事行為のみを行い、その国事行為はすべて内閣の助言と承認を必要とし、天皇は国政に関する権能を有しない、という条項にさかれています。憲法の最初に天皇についてこのようなことが書かれているということは、戦中の経験を踏まえ天皇の行動に強い制限を加えたということが考えられます。この日本国憲法には、民主主義の根幹を成す国会、国務大臣、国政選挙の、召集、任命、公示など、すべて内閣の助言と承認が必要とはいえ、第 1 条の主権在民からは奇異な感を受ける国事行為が含まれています。立憲君主の諸外国でも憲法にはこのような規定はありません。また、問題となる戦争の放棄と戦力を保持しないことを謳った第 9 条は日本側からの発案で、諸外国から批判のあった天皇制の存続のために持ち出された、というのが通説です。こうして日本国憲法が生まれ、それは平和憲法として、強大なアメリカによる西側世界の秩序の維持の下、幸いにも現在に至っています。

憲法に、天皇は日本国と日本国民統合の象徴、と書かれていますが、では、憲法に定められた、人が象徴とはどういうことでしょうか。国

旗や国歌のようなものは個別に法令により定められるもので、憲法に人が象徴と定められることは世界でも例がありません。象徴というのは誰からも特に強い異議の出ない、通常、国旗や国章など人以外のものが定められています。人の場合、すべての国民から異議が出ず、しかも尊敬される人格、という事になりますが、たとえ天皇であろうと個性がありますので、このような権威を保つには直接的な発言は控えられます。現代の民主主義国家のリーダーである首相や大統領は、不断に雄弁にものを語る必要があります。国民も誰でも積極的に発言出来、自己を実現することを目指しています。一方、天皇は何も発言しなくとも大きな地位が保障されています。

天皇制と民主主義は完全に矛盾した概念です。こうした説明の出来ない矛盾を放置することは、国民の論理的思考の発展に大変悪い影響を与えるものであると思います。

注1：宮内庁 HP 内、宮内庁関係予算の推移表、他より算出

注2：2009 年 11 月実施の NHK 世論調査より

注 3：天皇は初期から神道との関係が深く、また明治期に宗教面で神話上の天照大神が神道の最高神として統一されると、政府により、その子孫とされていた天皇を神そのものという位置に置く国家的状況（国家神道）が作り上げられました。戦後、政教分離が行われましたが、天皇が宗教の中心としての存在であるという意識は強いものがありますし、その背景は万世一系の血筋を受けた神性から来ています。

注 4：日本では世間と社会の違いは明確ではありませんが、両者には違いがあります。日本では江戸時代の武家政権から明治時代の近代国家体制へ急激に転換したために、それまでの閉鎖的な村意識や狭いコミュニティーで生活していた町人の意識が、そのまま社会の範囲にま

で拡大されて残ったものと考えられます。世間とはこの同一感を引き
ずったクローズな人間関係のことです。一般的に世間は権威に弱く、
人と違うことに強い抵抗感を持ちます。
社会とは市民意識を持った人々の集まりで、自立と意識の範囲はより
広いものがあります。

September 2017

Brief history of the author

Eizo Nishio: b.1953, Tokyo. / Graduated from the Faculty of Economics, Sophia University, Tokyo, and studied Social Sciences at Waseda University, Tokyo. / The author of *20/21C ART BOOKS: A Bibliography of Artists and Art Movements in the 20th and 21st Centuries*, *19C ART BOOKS: A Bibliography of Artists and Art in the 19th Century*, *Eizo Nishio: Sculptures & Drawings 2011-2014*, *Eizo Nishio: Paintings. Square and Long Rectangle*, and many other books.

Eizo Nishio: 1953 年東京生まれ。／上智大学経済学部卒業。早稲田大学社会科学部中退。／著書に *20/21C ART BOOKS: A Bibliography of Artists and Art Movements in the 20th and 21st Centuries*, *19C ART BOOKS: A Bibliography of Artists and Art in the 19th Century*, *Eizo Nishio: Sculptures & Drawings 2011-2014*, *Eizo Nishio: Paintings. Square and Long Rectangle*, 他多数。

ISBN 978-4-909594-01-3

Art & Books Publishers, Tokyo
www.artbibliography.com